Going by Train

by Susan Ashley

Reading consultant: Susan Nations, M.Ed., author/literacy coach/consultant

WEEKLY WR READER®
EARLY LEARNING LIBRARY
Somerset Co. Library
Bridgewater, NJ 08807

Please visit our web site at: **www.earlyliteracy.cc**
For a free color catalog describing Weekly Reader® Early Learning Library's
list of high-quality books, call 1-877-445-5824 (USA) or 1-800-387-3178 (Canada).
Weekly Reader® Early Learning Library's fax: (414) 336-0164.

Library of Congress Cataloging-in-Publication Data

Ashley, Susan.
    Going by train / by Susan Ashley.
        p. cm. — (Going places)
    Includes bibliographical references and index.
    Contents: Passenger trains — The fastest trains — Freight trains — Train power.
    ISBN 0-8368-3732-0 (lib. bdg.)
    ISBN 0-8368-3837-8 (softcover)
    1. Railroads—Trains—Juvenile literature. [1. Railroads—Trains.] I. Title.
TF148.A72 2003
385'.37—dc21   2003045009

This edition first published in 2004 by
Weekly Reader® Early Learning Library
330 West Olive Street, Suite 100
Milwaukee, WI 53212 USA

Copyright © 2004 by Weekly Reader® Early Learning Library

Art direction: Tammy Gruenewald
Photo research: Diane Laska-Swanke
Editorial assistant: Erin Widenski
Cover and layout design: Katherine A. Goedheer

Photo credits: Cover, title, pp. 4, 5, 13, 16, 19 © Gary J. Benson; pp. 6, 9, 18 © Kim Karpeles;
p. 7 Map courtesy of Amtrak; p. 8 © Gibson Stock Photography; pp. 10, 12, 20 © Ulrich Tutsch;
p. 11 © Eugene G. Schulz; pp. 14, 15, 17 © Gregg Andersen; p. 21 Courtesy of Transrapid
International-USA, Inc.

Printed in the United States of America

1 2 3 4 5 6 7 8 9 07 06 05 04 03

Table of Contents

This passenger train, called the "Desert Wind," takes people across the desert to Nevada and California.

Passenger Trains

Have you ever traveled on a train? Every day, all over the world, trains take people where they need to go. Trains that carry people are called passenger trains.

Many people take trains to work. Trains that bring people from the suburbs to the city are called commuter trains. Commuter trains reduce traffic on the highways.

This commuter train is called the Metra. People ride it to and from Chicago.

The elevated train in Chicago is called "the el."

Some large cities have subways or elevated trains that can take people quickly from one end of the city to the other. Subways are trains that run in tunnels underground. Elevated trains run on tracks above the street.

Trains can also take people long distances. In the United States, Amtrak trains carry passengers from city to city, from state to state, and all across the country! A route map shows where each train stops.

This Amtrak route map shows train routes between major cities in the Midwest.

A conductor shows passengers where to board the train.

Passengers board an Amtrak train at a train station. They can buy their tickets at the station before they board the train. The train conductor helps passengers find their seats. When the train is ready to go, a whistle blows!

Long-distance passenger trains have special cars. There are observation cars for watching the scenery. In dining cars, meals are served at tables, just like at a restaurant. There are even sleeping cars with beds.

This old-fashioned lounge car has large, comfortable seats where passengers can relax during their journey.

This high-speed passenger train has just pulled into the station. There are many high-speed trains in Europe.

The Fastest Trains

The world's fastest trains are in Europe and Japan. These high-speed passenger trains have their own tracks, so other trains will not slow them down. The tracks have few curves, so the trains can run at top speeds. Some of these trains are called "bullet trains."

The shape of these trains adds to their speed. The trains are streamlined. Streamlined objects are narrow and smooth. They come almost to a point at the end. This reduces air resistance and allows the trains to go very fast.

This "bullet train" in Japan has a streamlined shape. The train is as fast as it looks!

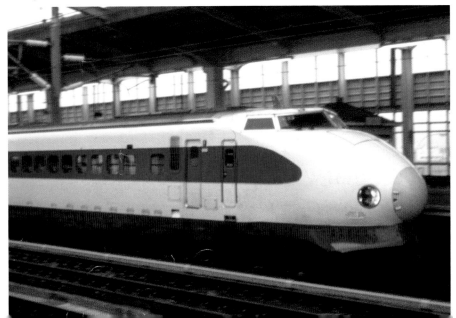

The TGV trains in France are some of the fastest trains in the world.

The TGV is a high-speed train in France. The letters stand for three French words meaning "very fast train." The TGV zooms down the track at 186 miles (300 kilometers) per hour. Japan's fastest trains are called "bullet trains" because of their speed and shape.

Freight Trains

A freight train carries goods instead of people. Many of the objects in your home traveled on a train at one time. Freight trains can have many cars. Some have more than one hundred cars! There are different types of freight cars.

Freight trains are often very long. They carry goods from coast to coast and all over the country.

Freight in a boxcar is loaded through these sliding doors.

A boxcar carries items packed in boxes, like computers or televisions. A boxcar looks like a large, steel box with sliding doors on each side. Freight is loaded into the car through these doors. The freight in a boxcar stays dry.

A hopper car carries loose loads, like gravel or sand. A hopper car is open on the top. Freight is loaded through the top of the car and unloaded through an opening at the bottom. The ends of a hopper car are slanted so the freight can pour out of the bottom easily.

A hopper car is open on the top, and the ends of a hopper car are slanted.

Tank cars are round. They are designed to carry liquids.

A tank car holds liquids. A tank car might carry milk or gasoline. A tank car is round and shaped like a tank. Tank cars have special linings to keep their contents warm or cold.

There are many other types of freight cars. Refrigerator cars keep fruits and vegetables fresh. Flatcars have no sides and can carry big logs and even tractors. The next time you see a freight train, look closely at the cars. Can you guess what is inside?

Fresh food is carried in refrigerator cars like this one. These cars act like your refrigerator at home and keep food cool so it won't spoil.

This engineer is riding in a 1923 steam engine. He uses controls inside the engine to make the train stop, go, and change speed.

Train Power

All trains need power to make them go. Most trains are pulled by an engine at the front of the train. Some trains have an engine at the back, pushing the train along the track. An engineer uses controls inside the engine to drive the train.

The earliest trains used steam engines. Steam engines were noisy and dirty. Most trains today are pulled by diesel engines. Some freight trains are so long, they need more than one diesel engine to pull them!

This train is being pulled by a steam engine. Trains like this were common a hundred years ago.

The power for this electric train comes from the cable above the train.

Electric trains use electricity to power the engines. The electricity comes from a cable above the train or from a third rail that runs along the track. Electric trains are fast and very quiet.

Someday we may ride in trains that are pulled along by magnetic power! People continue to think of new ideas to make trains faster and save energy.

Someday, people may travel in high-speed magnetic trains like this train being tested in Germany.

Glossary

commuter — a person who travels back and forth between a suburb and a city

elevated — raised above the ground

freight — goods carried from one place to another

resistance — a force that slows something down

route — a course of travel or regular round of stops

slanted — at an angle, not straight

streamlined — having a smooth, narrow form

suburb — an area or town close to a city

For More Information

Books

Heap, Christine. *Big Books of Trains*. New York: DK Publishing, Inc., 1998.

Hill, Lee Sullivan. *Trains*. Minneapolis: Lerner Publications, 2003.

Simon, Seymour. *Seymour Simon's Book of Trains*. New York: Harper Collins, 2002.

Stille, Darlene. *Freight Trains*. Minneapolis: Compass Point Books, 2002.

Web Sites

Amtrak Photo Gallery
www.amtrak.com/press/photogallery-copy.html
Photos of long-distance trains

Rochester Institute of Technology Model Railroad Club
www.ritmrc.org/railroad/paintdiagrams/freight.htm
Pictures of different types of freight cars

Train Terms
www.bytrain.org/redbarinfo/kids/trainterms.html
Train terms

Index